Children's imagination

Children's imagination
creativity under
our noses

URSULA
KOLBE

PEPPINOT PRESS

Copyright © Ursula Kolbe, 2014

First published in 2014 by Peppinot Press

PO Box 1775, Byron Bay NSW, 2481, Australia
Email: info@peppinotpress.com.au
Web: www.peppinotpress.com.au

Photography by Ursula Kolbe except: Vanessa Anderson (pp. 11, 17);
Susan Carrasco (p. 31a); Anika Ekholm Barrios (pp. 9, 30, 60);
Jennie Burrows (p. 51); Melanie Feddersen (pp. viii, 8, 72f);
Alison Free (pp. 33, 78); Lisa Hoelzl (p. 42); Karin Kolbe (p. 25, 79, 89a);
Tania McCartney (p. 28c); Genevieve McCrea (pp. 14, 15, 26, 27);
Janet Robertson (p. 83); Roslyn Savage (p. 22b); Madeleine Scott (p. 58);
Susan Whelan (pp. 12, 13, 20, 21, 23, 107); Tania Wursig (pp. 54, 55, 59, 63).

Permission has been kindly granted to use words from Susan Whelan on
pp. 17-18, 29-30, 44-5 and 59-61; and Janet Robertson on pp. 82-3.

Front cover: Drawing, felt-tip pen, Floria (5).
Back cover: Drawing, Aden (4).

Cover and text design by i2i Design
Set in 10/14pt Miramar

Printed in China by 1010 Printing International Limited

National Library of Australia Cataloguing-in-Publication entry
Author: Kolbe, Ursula, author.
Title: Children's imagination : creativity under our noses / Ursula Kolbe.
ISBN: 9780975772232 (paperback)
Subjects: Creation (Literary, artistic, etc.)
          Imagination in children.
Dewey Number: 155.4133

To Rosemary Darville

Acknowledgements

This book exists because of the generosity of children and their families
who welcomed me into their homes, shared anecdotes and photographs, and
allowed me to observe, take photographs and borrow children's drawings.
As this project stretched over years due to unforeseen circumstances, the
extra time allowed me to see some children more than once—opportunities
for which I am most grateful. My warmest thanks to all.

Special thanks go to Susan Whelan for providing another dimension to the
manuscript and for so unfailingly and patiently sticking by me and supporting
me through various drafts.

To Pauline Baker go my warmest thanks for her constant encouragement,
inspired suggestions and belief in the project. I am indebted to Janet Robertson
for her invaluable contribution. For their enthusiastic support and
contributions I warmly thank Jennie Burrows, Gerda Gamper, Dr. Alison Free,
Anne Fritz and Bronwyn Richens. Special thanks go also to Wendy Shepherd
and Dr. Cynthia à Beckett for their insightful comments.

To my editor Dr. Jeremy Steele, I am again deeply grateful, and I give special
thanks to Melanie Feddersen for her beautiful design. As always, though, my
deepest thanks go to my publisher, my daughter Karin Kolbe, for holding fast
to her wish for a third title to complete our trilogy about young children.

Contents

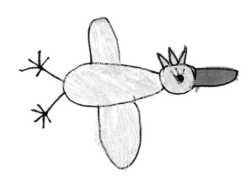

'I am enough of an artist to draw freely upon my imagination. Imagination is more important than knowledge. Knowledge is limited. Imagination encircles the world.'

Albert Einstein

Introduction

First, a chance happening that captures beautifully how I see creativity.

Michael (barely three) had just gone outside with me 'to look at things'. Almost immediately two brightly hued, glossy leaves fell in front of us, and Michael pounced on them. Swiftly rearranging them to form a V in his hand, he turned to look at me triumphantly and said: 'Flower!' He had taken two things and created a third, something original, something of value. The very essence of creativity.

Happily my camera caught the moment—as I suspect Michael wanted.

'Flower!'

What sparks children's imagination? What inspires their ideas? Can we discover what spurs their innovation and ingenuity? And what can we do to nourish and support their creative thinking?

My starting point for finding answers to these questions was to collect anecdotes about children's imaginative thinking from what families could tell me, as well as from my own observations in children's homes.

What triggers to the imagination could I find these children using? What if I shook my 'tree of anecdotes' to see what else might fall out? Could I detect common features worth sharing with others? I believe that I have, and this book is the result. It presents a distillation of many observations of children's imaginative and creative thinking from infancy to ten years. I hope it reassures parents that by allowing ample time for imaginative play they are doing their best for their children. I hope it supports teachers who want to create imaginative learning environments in which they can share in children's wonderment, as educator Cynthia à Beckett suggests, rather than being focussed on outcomes that limit possibilities for imaginative thinking.[1]

My focus is on how children use visual language as a means of inquiry, as a playful way to imagine new possibilities and make their ideas visible, and I hope that the vignettes will help you to understand better what they do and make. As artist and Reggio Emilia educator Vea Vecchi remarks, what's involved is a process of thinking simultaneously with 'hands, sensibilities and brain' with 'the imagination as a unifying element'.[2]

Part One relates anecdotes of children's imaginative thinking in action and describes unexpected provocations that piqued children's curiosity and spurred innovation.

Part Two reflects on what can be learnt from the anecdotes and looks at how you can nourish and support children's creative endeavours.

Introducing Susan Whelan

Offering a parent's perspective on some of the anecdotes is Susan Whelan, writer and mother of three, who shares my deep interest in children's imagination and creative thinking. We trust that this book will inspire you to make your own discoveries about children and find out more about their passions and ideas. And perhaps unlock and rekindle the creativity in you.

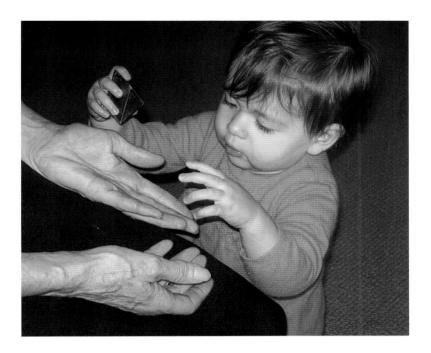

A tender moment

Recently I witnessed a little scene that captures the spirit that I hope pervades this book.

Something is underway. Fifteen-month-old Pip holds a toy block (a triangular-shaped one she found in a basket of blocks), while Gerda, a family friend sitting beside her, quietly watches. Could this be a toddler's version of 'show and tell'—except that the telling is done with gestures rather than words? What might Pip be 'telling'?

Gerda told me that during the morning Pip had constantly played with a triangular block—one smaller and more familiar to her than this one. Is she possibly feeling a resemblance between the remembered one and this new one now in her hands? If I hadn't been studying recent findings about the remarkable workings of babies' minds, I wouldn't have thought of asking this. Now, I wonder.

Whatever the reasons, it's clear that Pip wants to show her find. The desire to communicate and share is innate, and from birth humans seek companions. What is so moving here is the feeling of mutuality between Pip and Gerda: both are in the same companionable space. Without a word, something is being communicated. All too often we adults feel the need to label, to continually teach, whereas close attention and companionable silence are often more valuable. Valuable because then *anything* can happen.

Why do I see something special in this seemingly ordinary moment? Perhaps it's because Pip's *presentation* represents the beginning of a creative act, while Gerda's interest embodies the kind of support that creativity needs.

'Tunnels!'

When three-year-old Michael placed three felt-tip pen lids side by side, he suddenly saw something new. 'Tunnels!' he exclaimed delightedly. Watching him play with his tunnels, I realised that here was another moment that revealed something important. Young children's ability to see the extraordinary in the ordinary—to make connections between unusual things that seem unrelated—is an ability that I want to bring to light in this book.

Making connections, Ellen Galinsky writes, is an 'essential skill', a key part of learning.[3] And at the heart of creativity, as some of my stories will show, is making unusual connections.

part one

What sparks children's imagination?

Here, then, is my 'tree of anecdotes'—the stories and observations that say something to me. I've grouped them into sections that each highlight a key aspect of what seems to spark children's thinking.

I say 'seems' because we can never really be certain of what fires someone else's thinking and imagination. However, looking closely at what children do, and trying to understand what captures their interest and why, can be extremely rewarding for both observer and children alike.

The sections follow in a sequence that increases in complexity. At the end of each one, Susan Whelan and I talk about the key aspects that the anecdotes reveal.

'The imagination is the power of the mind over the possibilities of things.'

Wallace Stevens

Found surprises

These anecdotes reveal children's responses to objects they happened to find, and how these fired their imagination.

In some examples found objects become props in make-believe play. In others, they become a means for children to give voice to their interests.

Found objects are full of possibilities. Not only intriguing to the eye and hand, they speak to the imagination. They present challenges. Running through each of the anecdotes seems to be an unspoken question: *What can I do with this?*

Making soup

After gathering seedpods, twigs and leaves from the ground, Luna, barely three, asks her mother for a bowl—and with that, her make-believe cooking starts. 'I'm making soup!' she says, stirring her finds. *Just* play? The imaginary begins in play. Through making new connections and pretending that her found objects in the bowl are now food, Luna is thinking imaginatively. Substituting one thing for another like this, developmental psychologists have shown, is the starting point for learning to think abstractly.

'I'm making soup!' says Luna (just 3).

Tower of Magic, wood pieces, glued, painted, and adorned with toy plastic animals, Luna (5).

Over the next few years, Luna continues to gather all manner of interestingly shaped objects. By age five, her ability to select challenging shapes is well developed. She has a whole box of found treasures that she likes rummaging through. 'Often a piece reminds her of something,' her father tells me. 'She'll say, "This looks like ..." and then she'll start making something. She's been gluing leftover pieces of wood together since she was three.'

A bejewelled crocodile

Eyeing the empty containers after a take-away meal, five-year-old Cedar is instantly attracted to one that opens and shuts. Manipulating it with both hands, she sees its potential: 'Look! It can be a snappy crocodile! We can put some hand thing to go on like this, and green stuff and then you can go *Snap! Snap! Snap!*' The box has already become alive in her hands.

Using a large marker, Cedar quickly adds green markings.

> Dad, I'm going to make a tongue for my croc.
>
> *How are you going to do that?*
>
> I'm going to cut it out [of paper]. You have to have red. I'd like this to be a beauty crocodile!
>
> *How will you do that?*
>
> Stick jewels on her and beads and stuff, so that's why she's a beauty croc like Beauty and the Beast. I can make her a spiky croc. Now I'm going to put eyes on her—scary eyes! ... *A-ha-ha-ha! HAAAR!*

Beauty crocodile, polystyrene container, glitter, tiny ornaments, craft matchsticks, Cedar (5).

To make something that didn't exist before *that you've designed yourself* is wonderfully satisfying. By making something playfully 'scary', Cedar may also be dealing with scariness. Perhaps by beautifying the crocodile with jewels, so taming it, Cedar allows herself to explore scariness safely.

Inventions

'In our home,' said Vanessa, mother of six-year-old Regan, 'we have two bins; one for general rubbish and one for recycling stuff like plastic bottles, cardboard and paper. Most mornings I'm very busy cleaning up the house before we go out, and I usually give Regan what she needs for drawing to keep her occupied. One particular morning she seemed quite busy, but after a while I decided to check on what she was doing. That's when I found that she'd emptied the recycling bin all over the floor. I was annoyed at first because she'd made such a mess, but then I thought better of it.' Here's a snippet from their conversation.

> I'm making inventions. This one's a puffer ship.' (Shows a pizza box covered with odds and ends from the recycling bin.)
>
> *What does it do?*
>
> It goes on water and it has rules and the rules are: No boys allowed, no bats and no walking spiders at night!

Sure enough, she had drawn these 'rules' on the pizza box. Like most six-year-olds, she's well aware of rules made by parents and teachers, but how empowering it is to make up her own rules aboard an imaginary ship!

ABOVE: No boys allowed, no bats and no walking spiders. Regan didn't write the rules, but rather drew images to represent them.

LEFT: Puffer ship with notice about on-board rules, cardboard container, paper, felt-tip pen, Regan (6).

Collage delights

The look and feel of various scraps of paper, tissue, fabric and lace can speak evocatively to the imagination. When you start handling them and putting them into unexpected combinations, you begin to see them differently. Making a collage is much more than simply cutting and pasting. Choosing what to use and where to place each piece is the exciting part. Choosing gives you ideas, and you can always change them midway.

Elizabeth gets ideas from whatever's on hand. She selects bits and pieces, gathers them into piles, and then starts seeing what she can make. It's a favourite activity that she's continued to enjoy over several years.

Patchwork collage, tissue paper, fabric, coloured paper, Elizabeth (5).
'At the time I was trying my hand at making patchwork,' said her mother,
'so I guess that influenced her thinking.'

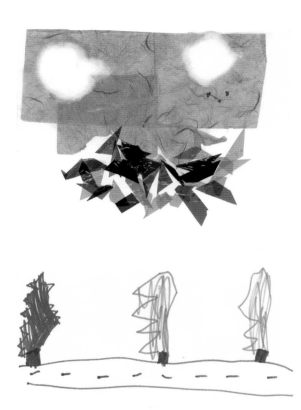

It's raining, sparkling cellophane pieces, dull slate-blue tissue, fluffy cotton balls, felt-tip pen, Elizabeth (8). A lovely mix of collage and drawing.

Birthday cake, tissue paper, felt-tip pens, white and coloured paper, Elizabeth (8). Another mix of collage and drawing.

A house takes shape

The desire to build a structure that stands and *stays up* is a powerful one. But how and where to start? Ten-year-old Matthew instinctively begins by letting the shapes and feel of scrap materials speak to his hands. What do these materials want to be? What do they suggest?

A metal strip, firm yet bendable, invites Matthew (10) to explore various possibilities.

Can the metal piece be used for a roof? 'I don't know how I'm going to get it to stand up,' says Matthew. Yes, a good example of what happens when you're not following a set design and have to face uncertainty and take risks. Learning not to be afraid of taking risks extends your scope enormously.

The metal strip has now become a fence and the building is taking shape. Each step involves solving unique structural problems.

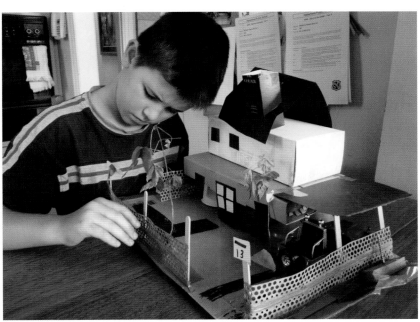

House with carport, cardboard, containers, metal, Matthew (10).

Stones

Ten-year-old Tyler, a boy with Down's Syndrome, has a passion for collecting and handling stones. 'For years he's been attracted to stones and rocks of all kinds,' his mother tells me.

Of course we need to be mindful that building with stones requires supervision, but I include this vignette because I learned so much from it. Tyler's intense concentration on building his cluster of stones (which lasted nearly half an hour) says much to me. It says something powerful about children's desire to make and to build. Equally it says something about the desire to connect with nature—a desire that sadly is often unfulfilled today.

It may only look like a heap of stones and rocks, but look again. I see a sort of cairn or a mound. I'm not suggesting that a cairn was Tyler's intention but he's certainly building a mound.

Talking with
Susan Whelan

uk Looking back at the anecdotes in this section, it seems that despite differences in age, ability and materials, each child invented what was, in essence, a 'tower of magic'—to borrow the title of Luna's construction. They discovered ways to *transform* the things they'd found.

sw Yes, and as a parent, getting an insight into children's ideas and interests through the things they collect and make is fascinating.

uk I recall Vanessa [the 'puffer ship' mother] saying: 'In the past, when we used a craft book to do activities together, it usually ended up in a great deal of frustration. I'd encourage Regan to make something, say a fish, as the exercise in the book intended, but she'd have no desire or intention to make a fish—and if she did, it was just to please me. Now the recycling bin, with added extras like pens, scissors, tape and glue, gives her the freedom to create what she wants, when she wants to.'

sw As a parent, it can be difficult to let go—not to feel that we have to be constantly guiding, offering suggestions, and trying to draw the maximum learning potential from every moment. I've also often been left feeling frustrated by the proliferation of books and websites emphasising step-by-step craft projects with predetermined outcomes that don't let children think for themselves.

uk Thinking for themselves is, of course, exactly what making things with objects like pieces of wood they've collected encourages children to do.

sw Collecting things seems to be particularly fascinating for some children. Like Luna, my daughter Elizabeth will often find something that appeals to her visually—a leaflet, an image in a magazine, a scrap of material, a button, a postcard. She collects these things like a bowerbird*, making an ever-changing display on her table or her bedroom door. Sometimes she uses bits to make something, but really she's surrounding herself with things that spark her imagination. Someone referred to Elizabeth's display as 'a holding space for reflection'. I love those words!

uk I think putting pictures into a 'holding space' is a lovely thing to do. It's something artists and designers do all the time. I wonder whether children

Now the recycling bin, with added extras like pens, scissors, tape and glue, gives her the freedom to create what she wants, when she wants to.

* The bowerbird is native to Australia and New Guinea. Males build a decorated, bower-like structure to attract females. The term is also used informally in Australia to describe someone who collects miscellaneous objects.

who whizz through dozens of digital pictures—exciting as it may be at the time—get the same satisfaction as a child who handles and collects real things. Perhaps the answer is to find a balance between real experiences and digital ones.

sw We forget how enchanting very simple things can be for children—if we allow them time to explore.

uk Yes, experiencing things that feed the imagination, like collecting raindrops to make a silvery puddle in a nasturtium leaf cup as I loved to do as a child, can be more valuable than the business of making something.

sw I think that adults sometimes become too focussed on children achieving an end-result, even though the process of creating is just as important, if not more so. The process can also be a way of dealing with and expressing emotions, like uncertainty, fear, excitement or love.

uk And the creative process always has a playful character. Play is part of the process at any level.

sw And enjoying problem-solving is part of it too.

uk Yes! You can certainly see problem-solving in Matthew's *House with carport*. Figuring out which materials best suited his purpose, and experimenting with ways to keep the parts balanced and upright certainly gave him great satisfaction. And in a different way you can see something similar in Tyler's stone pile. Although Tyler has few words for expressing feelings and ideas, the intensity of his effort in building the pile speaks volumes. You could sense his excitement and pride in using his hands and his strength to shift the stones. He knew exactly what kind of materials best challenged him.

• • •

You could sense his excitement and pride in using his hands and his strength to shift the stones.

The anecdotes in *Found surprises* show how resourceful children can be in finding new things with which to challenge themselves. Picasso once said, 'I do not seek, I find.' I think he was being more than a little disingenuous; clearly he was an intensely curious seeker all his life. However, he probably meant that for him, an artist ever open to surprise and ready to take risks, the sheer act of *finding* was in itself a creative act.

Let's look now at another aspect that captures and holds children's attention: *spaces* that allow thoughts to roam.

Enticing
spaces

An *empty* space can excite the imagination. Whether it's floor space, space inside a box, or simply a blank sheet of paper, sheer emptiness—if conditions are right— can invite action. Let's look at some examples.

A garden

When I heard how five-year-old Jonas (who seldom drew) had been galvanised into making an unusually large drawing simply because he had the chance to draw on cardboard packaging sheets, I knew I had to write about it. Clearly Jonas saw the cardboard sheets as an exciting invitation; the chance to draw on a large scale was irresistible. Here is his large composite drawing—one that was to be a breakthrough for him in regaining interest in drawing.

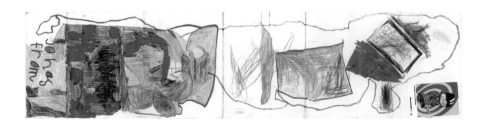

Garden, five sections, felt-tip pens on cardboard packaging sheets, Jonas (5). Jonas loves being in the garden with his mother. The five panels represent the garden, himself in the pool and his mother watering plants.

Raiding the button jar

Floor space has particular delights: how wonderful it can be to tip a jar of buttons onto a mat on the floor—as long as the children no longer put things in their mouths! Sitting amidst buttons, becoming part of a button-world of colour, is a magical experience for four-year-old Jasmine. For seven-year-old Elizabeth, it's a marvellous opportunity to select and arrange subtle gleaming colours into something poetic.

Jasmine (4) seems transfixed by the beauty of contrasting colours, shapes and textures.

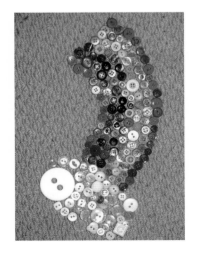

Rainbow with cloud, Elizabeth (7).

A passion for buses

Again on a floor, this time drawing combines with play with toy buses. Six-year-old Tom has a longstanding fascination with buses and their routes. Bus timetables, bus maps—he collects anything to do with buses, particularly the ones he and his family regularly use. His collection of toy buses is a prized possession. Presented with a large sheet of heavy paper on the floor and a thick black felt-tip pen, he's immediately inspired to draw roads and bus lanes for his fleet.

Road with pedestrian crossing and zigzag warning sign, black felt-tip pen, Tom (6).

'I think he becomes so engaged because this kind of drawing connects with his real world, his passions,' said his mother.

A monorail

Here is another setup on a floor that took six-year-old Matthew W. several hours to construct. It's easy to see that having the freedom to occupy this large space was vital to his creation of an imaginary world and a story.

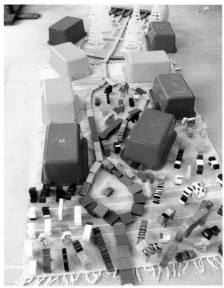

Monorail going through mountains, a desert and a forest, wooden blocks, wooden animals, plastic containers and cones, Matthew W. (6).

Colour music

Now to a completely different way to play with space: subdividing a sheet of paper into smaller spaces and filling them with arrangements of lines, shapes and colours. Pattern-makers love repetition. They delight in inventing games with lines, shapes and colours that follow rules of their own making, and constantly seek ways to add complications to increase the challenge. In the following web of repeated spiralling lines (below left), six-year-old Zara seems interested in seeing where the repetitions will take her.

Felt-tip and metallic pens, Zara (6). Rather than pursue a definite outcome, Zara seems to be generating a host of ideas for future exploration.

Felt-tip and metallic pens, Zara (6). A symphony of pinks and purples. Another self-invented pattern-making game, again with repeating lines—this time, mostly straight ones.

Making cards

Small, even tiny, spaces can also attract children's attention. Among the many small things that children love to make are cards: birthday cards, get-well cards, thank-you cards and so on. It seems that folding a blank sheet of paper to make something with four sides that can also *stand up*, has special appeal.

Cards by Cedar, Zara, Robbie, Floria. Made for specific people, these cards are not *just* cards— they are genuine gifts.

The very shape and size of a card seem to inspire a different kind of drawing. I think it's because being small, a card imposes a certain constraint on drawing that appeals to some children. Far from limiting creativity, self-imposed constraints often inspire children to try new things.

Roads, river and a highway

In contrast to the small spaces on cards, these photographs show what a long narrow sheet of paper on a floor can inspire. Over the years ten-year-old twins Michael and Matthew have jointly made several large drawings of streets for their toy cars.

When they were younger, they used to go for walks with their mother along local streets, pointing out features such as roundabouts, bridges, parking lots, names on shop fronts and so on. It was easier then (and involved fewer squabbles) when each worked on a separate sheet before sticking them together. Now they work collaboratively—the drawings becoming ever more detailed and intricate.

Detail, *Two towns*.

A mix of remembered and imagined places, the twins' drawings over the years reflect their changing interests and experiences. 'It's almost as if they're constructing a mind-map of their own life,' their mother commented.

Two towns, black felt-tip pen, Michael and Matthew (10). 'We did it over two days. First we drew the big highway going through, then the river, then the streets. And then the details—parks and things. We named the streets. This is our most advanced one so far. It's about our sixth or seventh!'

Imagined interior spaces

Inspired by a very small square piece of paper, six-year-old Joshua seems to be engaging with *what ifs*: what would it be like in a tiny cabin in the ocean's depths? The drawing shows an enclosed space that also seems to function like a house. Joshua's words about 'battleship people and monkey bars inside for the kids to play on' suggest a well-planned dwelling space.

A very small square inspires a surprisingly detailed drawing.

Inside a ship under water, very deep, felt-tip pen, Joshua (6).

For ten-year-old Ella, constructing miniature interiors from paper has been a long-standing interest.

'One day I was bored so I decided to make little houses and I made little kitchens and bathrooms and I put little toys inside them. And sometimes I'd pretend I was a designer. ... I just design them as I go. It comes to me as I go along,' Ella told me. Ever since she was about seven, when paper was the only material she had, Ella has been making interiors of tiny kitchens, bedrooms and bathrooms. At age ten she is still making them.

Interior, paper construction with toys, Ella (10). Ella's favourite part is 'putting all the detail in. I put in little knives and forks and make specific foods for the fridge ... normally I play with them.'

Talking with
Susan Whelan

uk When I first started writing about the enticements of space, I thought about places for children's thoughts to roam. But of course there's more to it. What you see in some anecdotes is that when children make things, they also create spaces for themselves to *be* in. A special place where they can pursue their own interests, where they feel free to be who they are, where their presence is somehow magnified.

sw Yes, and when Matthew built his monorail system he created a whole new world for himself—a space large enough to move around in. He loves to explain things, so when his constructions are finished, he often invites me to visit, taking me on a tour of what he's built and describing what each part means: 'These—he was pointing to the cylindrical blocks—are the engines. They go along the monorail track and stop at the stations—they were the upturned plastic containers. First they go through the mountains, the plastic cones, and then they go through the desert and forest where all the animals are.' And that was only half of his explanation!

uk But for Tom it was different; he wanted to recreate the buses and bus routes he travels on every day—part of the reality of his life close to the city.

sw You mentioned that you see the cards children make of their own accord as genuine gifts. I wonder if creating a card gives them a different sense of space. Maybe the appeal of a space inside a space, being able to open a card to reveal a second space, is part of the attraction.

uk Oh definitely! Miniature interior spaces particularly appeal to the imagination. I'm thinking of Joshua's underwater ship and Ella's paper interiors—ones she likes to play with. Imaginative play keeps cropping up.

sw Like the play with the monorail and the bus routes, or the twins' road map.

uk An interest that's lasted years. Wonderful that the twins have been able to persist with their ideas and develop them further. Helping to keep their interest alive, I think, was having extremely long pieces of paper to draw on—pieces that suggest some sort of journey in ways that a squarish rectangle can't. Also their previous drawings were still around for them to see and get ideas from.

A special place where they can pursue their own interests, where they feel free to be who they are, where their presence is somehow magnified.

sw I've always thought of time as another space that invites children to stretch their imagination. Knowing that they have enough time to develop their thoughts and plans over hours, even days, gives them the freedom to build on their ideas.

uk Yes, definitely. And what about outdoor space? In contrast to the indoor spaces we've been talking about, the vastness of outdoor space can have a very different effect on how we feel. The sights, sounds and smells, and the feeling of sunshine and breeze on the skin, all make you see things anew.

Making her own mark in this vast space, Luna (3) tries to make a found stick stand up in the damp sand.

Fairy, felt-tip pen, leaves, petals, glue, Sophia (6). Her grandmother's garden is a source of wonder for Sophia: a magical place for collecting petals and bits of greenery for making pictures.

• • •

Space to stretch out in or creep into—large, small, outside or inside—space *speaks* to the imagination. We've already been witness to examples of children's capacity for finding, making and using spaces to pursue ideas that matter to them. It's also worth noting that allowing enough uninterrupted and unhurried time gives them another 'space' to expand in.

Let's look now at the crucial element of companionship, and how it supports creativity. Creative thinking is often more likely to develop when you're in company with others.

Together in the moment

In this section I want to focus on companionable moments, those unexpected effortless times when harmony and a sense of mutuality pervade. That's when something special can happen.

Jasper's teacup

'Would you like a cup of tea, Noni?' asks three-year-old Jasper. He's playing with his toy kitchen while Noni, his step-grandmother, is cooking. *Yes, please, Jasper.* Jasper makes her a cup of tea in a pink teacup. *Delicious! Thank you, Jasper.* Just then a family friend, Roberta, arrives. 'Hello Berta—would you like a cup of tea too?' *Thanks Jasper, I'd love a cup of tea—with milk please.*

This pleasant little scene, with all players understanding their roles, is suddenly disrupted. Rummaging in his kitchen, Jasper discovers he doesn't have a cup for Roberta. Consternation!

Almost immediately, however, he brightens. Smiling broadly, he announces: 'Hey! I know: I'll draw one!' In solving his problem so rapidly, we're seeing not only how resourceful a young child can be, but also how the challenge revealed how important it was to Jasper to continue his scenario.

The idea of drawing a cup was spontaneous (though it may have been provoked by something seen in a children's television program—in which case, it's a good example of how children take ideas from anywhere to suit their own purposes). Luckily, having pen and paper close at hand and Roberta's encouraging eyes to support him, Jasper could speedily put his idea into practice: pretend tea, after all, can exist in any kind of pretend cup! And so his tea-party ended happily.

Typically, young children use circular shapes to stand for many different objects. In this case, the circular shape stands for the cup as well as a view into it from above, or just 'cupness' if you like. The short straight mark at right angles to the circular shape is interesting; Jasper tells Roberta that it's the cup's handle. It's an inventive solution to the graphic problem of depicting something that *protrudes* from another surface.

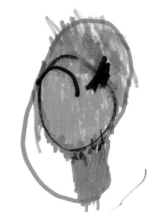

Teacup, felt-tip pen, Jasper (3).
The drawing *stands for* a cup rather than depicting one.

What birds have pink feathers?

This was the question that six-year-old Zara suddenly asked of five-year-old sister Cedar and their mother as they were walking home after a swim in the creek. It was the start of a lively conversation that led to dressing-up and play-acting, and finally, picture-making. But what had inspired Zara's question about pink feathers? Was it a moment when she noticed her pink sarong wafting about her shoulders? Did the fluttering pinkness suggest wings to her?

Answers about pink birds came quickly: 'Galahs,' suggested Cedar.* 'Flamingos,' added their mother, 'they have lots of pink.' That did it. 'I'm going to be a flamingo!' said Zara, flapping her sarong wings.

Enlarging on the theme of pinkness as they neared home, Zara asked, 'What pink clothes have I got?' She raced into the house and then emerged, despite the heat of the day, in a pink long-sleeved top, pink velvet leggings and the sarong. Pretending to be a flamingo on one leg she said, 'I know where flamingos live—Egypt!'

'What else do you know about Egypt?' her mother asked.

'There are camels, crocodiles, swallows and they have pyramids. I know how to draw a pyramid!'

*A galah is a pink-breasted cockatoo found in Australia.

A flamingo in Egypt, felt-tip pens, Zara (6). An imagined world on paper: a lovely amalgam of ideas from Zara, her sister and mother— all starting from an unexpected provocation.

Once at the kitchen table, Zara drew a pyramid. Beside it she drew a girl in red representing her sister Cedar, who by now had swathed herself in red finery, announcing, 'I'm an Egypt girl 'cos I've got a red dress on and that says you are Egypt.'

A palm tree in the picture emerged after this exchange.

> Mum, are there any trees in Egypt?
>
> *Not many, but I think they have palm trees.*
>
> Are they coconut palm trees?
>
> *I think they're date palm trees.*
>
> I'm just going to draw one tree because there aren't many.

Beneath a rainbow

Seven-year-old Naomi and I were admiring a drawing of a girl that Naomi had just made at the kitchen table. Glancing at me, a visiting family friend, she seemed to want me to suggest what she might do next. 'What if you cut her out?' I said.

Curious, Naomi decided to try. Soon the cutout drawing of a girl acquired a friend, a cat and a dog. Placing them on a patch of drawn grass, Naomi had a new idea: 'I need to make a rainbow!' She wasn't too sure how to make one that would arch over the group, but after a few attempts she made one large enough and cut it out. The next challenge was to find a way to make it hover above the group. Undaunted, after some experimentation Naomi managed to make a rainbow that arched over the group.

As so often happens, one idea led to another, and bit by bit a scene emerged, a scene that celebrates the idea of friendship—an enduring theme that pops up in so much of what children make.

It starts with a drawing ...

Naomi puts paste on a cardboard strip at the back of the figure.

Me and my friend.

The cutouts now stand on the grass.

Me and my friend and a cat and a dog, felt-tip pens, Naomi (7). Together the drawings became a little piece of theatre, a wordless story about friendship.

Story without end

Eight-year-old friends Persia and Sian were playing with some plasticine. It should have been soft and malleable, but being of poor quality, age had hardened it. I thought they wouldn't play for long with this crumbling stuff, yet how wrong I was! While the plasticine didn't allow them to make shapes of any complexity, it did enable them to make pieces to use as props as they acted out an evolving story about the comings and goings of some very tiny plastic dolls. As each new shape suggested another idea, so the often hilarious story continued.

Each inspired the other; and so the story continued to evolve.

Undoubtedly the story kept the action going. Of course it's preferable to provide children with the best quality materials we can afford; poor materials often limit what they can do. However, children are resourceful, and when they need to find alternative ways of doing things, limitations can be a spur to creativity.

Choochoo and Max go fishing

This is the title of eight-year-old Robbie's story about his two much-loved stuffed animals going to sea and their encounters with a monster and other perils they faced. He'd typed it on the family's computer. When he emailed it to his aunt, she suggested that he might make a book from it when he and his sister next came to stay.

Later their aunt told me that soon after they arrived, 'Robbie and I discussed how he'd do the illustrations. He was quite clear that he didn't want to draw them. As his story featured two stuffed animals, I suddenly thought he could photograph them instead. As we talked about this idea, Robbie excitedly mentioned the scenes in which they appear. We then realised he needed a list of scenes that he could actually set up. I left him to make the list, and about ten minutes later he produced it!'

Making the list of scenes.

The next step was for Robbie to talk about how he visualised the scenes. How did he think the monster might look, or the desert island that the animals discover? He quickly improvised scenery and props using whatever was at hand. A blue towel became the sea, a cardboard box the boat. Animating his story in three dimensions gave him a chance to reinvent the scenes he'd imagined. Planning how he would photograph them was a new challenge.

Photographing Choochoo and Max in the boat.

Setting up the confrontation between the animals and the sea monster.

Sea monster, 'I made it out of a helmet and a football and a piece of cloth. Then I stuck on the eyes and mouth,' said Robbie.

Robbie positions Choochoo and Max on the island (made from cushions). A volcano and trees are in the background.

Robbie and his sister review and select photographs for the book.

Sea monster.

The volcano on the island, (cloth-covered container with smoke drawn on paper scrap).

Inserting the photographs into Robbie's story was simple as the emailed story was already on file. Using a word processing program, Robbie and his aunt positioned the photographs in the appropriate spots. The file was then sent to a local colour photocopying service where it was printed and spiral-bound.

Of all the anecdotes in this book, this one contains the most sustained adult involvement—but with an adult only as co-explorer, helping to keep the momentum going, and assisting with technical advice when needed. Neither Robbie nor his aunt knew how things might unfold. Bringing the story to life was a journey of playful improvisation, excitement and discovery for both of them.

The camaraderie between the characters Choochoo and Max, particularly clear in their dialogue as they cheerfully battle against various dangers and problems, shows that their story is as much about friendship as the perennial conflict between good and evil.

Robbie shows his mother the finished book.

Inventing a family

Eight-year-old Mimi began making worry dolls after reading *Silly Billy* by Anthony Browne, a picturebook story about a little boy who worries about everything.[4] His grandmother gives him a set of Guatemalan worry dolls to put under his pillow at night so that they can worry for him while he sleeps. The diversion works. However he then realises that he has unfairly transferred all his worries to the dolls. So he makes more worry dolls for his first set of dolls, to alleviate *their* worries, and so on.

Once she'd started, Mimi continued to add ever more dolls to her family of adult and baby worry dolls for several weeks. Not only did they seem to become her companions, it became apparent to her mother that she was attributing to the dolls particular worries about people in her own life. 'I made a family, and wrote their names on the back,' was all she told me.

With inviting materials beside her, Mimi can't resist making yet more dolls—even when travelling in the car.

Worry dolls, Mimi (8). Coloured paddle-pop sticks, faces drawn with black felt-tip pen, glued-on clothes made from animal print paper, cellophane, and other materials.

When less is more

Now to something that couldn't be simpler. There were four of us at a table in the family living room: four-year-old Sammi, six-year-old Joshua, and in her high chair beside me, sixteen-month-old Sarah. Sammi and Joshua were both drawing invented worlds on paper, and Sarah clearly wanted to be busy too. A crayon didn't interest her, neither did a toy. 'Would a piece of paper do?' I suggested to her mother Gemma nearby. She remembered a packet of collected paper scraps, which she began emptying onto the table in front of us. When a few tiny red cellophane squares fluttered down, Sarah knew exactly what she wanted, and what followed was fascinating. She played with a single cellophane square in every possible way, investigating what it was and what she could do with it, all the while babbling most expressively to me. I responded with facial expressions, some words and the clicking of my camera. The unexpected beauty of a tiny *see-through* sparkling red square enchanted us both.

Sarah remained engrossed for seventeen minutes. No doubt having my attention helped, but she showed me yet again that very young children can persist in their explorations for surprising lengths of time when they want to investigate something that intrigues them. Play that's self-initiated and self-directed is usually the key, and in this instance Sarah had found a toy of her own making.

Serious play: like a scientist or artist, Sarah is intent on finding out what this tiny translucent object is and how her actions can change its appearance.

Talking with
Susan Whelan

sw The standout point for me in this section is the role of conversation. I love the way conversations simply evolved from whatever was happening—like when a question about pink feathers led to talking about Egypt! It really showed how ideas can flow.

uk Yes, when we're in the moment with children, they feel comfortable asking all sorts of questions. It's wonderful how freewheeling conversations can encourage imaginative thinking.

sw And through dialogue children can develop their ideas and think out loud about what they'll do next.

uk Talking to themselves is a good way to work things out too.

sw Sometimes of course, children do want a suggestion, like when they feel stuck for ideas.

uk Sure. I remember that when Naomi had drawn a girl, she seemed to want some sort of suggestion from me. But I was a bit stuck too. As a visitor, I didn't know what'd gone on before, so I was reluctant to suggest something that might backfire. I've found that children often disappear if they think the adult has some result in mind that they feel unsure about or don't like. However, my question, 'What if you cut her out?' aroused Naomi's curiosity. Okay, that doesn't always work, but curiosity often leads to action. Playfully asking 'I wonder' and 'What if' encourages a willingness to try things.

sw I've also found that questions that can't be answered with a simple yes or no help to continue the conversation.

uk And asking questions, like *What can you tell me about ... ?*

sw When kids have ideas but don't know how to sequence them or where to start, it helps to talk things over with someone else. When Robbie and his aunt talked about making a list of the scenes he wanted to photograph for his book, it really helped him to break down a complex task.

uk On the other hand, trust in children's resourcefulness and creativity is important too. Finding your own solutions to self-imposed challenges is very satisfying. It's wonderful that Jasper could create a teacup in his own way, and that the girls with the old plasticine could overcome its limitations by making up a story.

sw And Sarah's story shows how a very young child can be fascinated by a piece of material that can be handled and twisted and scrunched in a myriad ways. A cardboard box is another example of something with many possibilities. I get so frustrated by advertisements telling parents that we must progress our children through a series of 'age-appropriate' steps, and all of them depend on buying new materials and products. I think we can easily end up oversimplifying our children's experiences, and that can make it make it difficult for them to make spontaneous discoveries and connections which lead them into creative thinking.

• • •

Whether with real people or imaginary ones, the sense of companionship in the various anecdotes in this section was certainly a key feature in encouraging children to persist with their explorations and ideas. As we've noticed earlier, the ability to persist with something is an important element in the creative process. For children joy in overcoming challenges *by themselves* is usually reward enough; however, it does help to feel that someone close by— whether sibling, friend or adult—is also interested.

The following section is devoted to children's graphic exploration. Drawing already features in previous sections, of course, but now it's time to look at it more closely.

Perched on a staircase—a favourite spot—two friends swop ideas about making tiny cloth dolls.

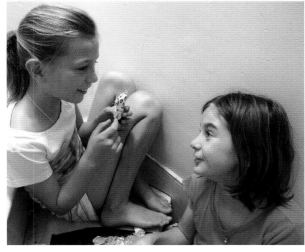

Graphic exploration: a universal form of play

The urge to draw appears to be universal. Beginning with early playful mark-making, children develop an understanding that mere lines and shapes on paper can stand for real objects and events, words and ideas *beyond* the drawing surface.

It's a profoundly important development. Their rapt faces and the stillness of their bodies when they're engrossed in drawing tell us that something significant is going on.

The act of making marks on paper—often misunderstood and undervalued—offers children such an extraordinary springboard for the imagination that it warrants a whole separate section.

Something is happening

When I first met Michael (just three) I offered him paper and some felt-tip pens. He looked at me expectantly. Needing to establish quickly that I had no agenda other than that he enjoy himself, I said, 'Ah Michael, why don't you see what the pen will do?'

Immediately he began covering some sheets of paper with a variety of markings; on others he delighted in making large circular arm movements that produced large shapes, and on a final sheet he drew a series of straight lines and dots. Then something else happened. Rapidly drawing over some of his blue lines, he excitedly began a running commentary: 'Hey, it's getting darker! Can you guess what's underneath? Dots! It's getting even darker! Do you know what's under it again? Dots! So much dark!' Indeed, dark patches now hid his dots.

Hey, it's getting darker!

Michael's investigations lasted over half an hour, and it was evident that that he not only wanted to share his observations with me, but was also interested in what I saw and thought. At first glance his mark-making may seem to have little to do with imaginative thinking, but his response to the effect of his later unexpected marks ('So much dark!') suggests that he was giving a meaning to the patches he'd made. If you pause to think about it, darkness is a notable phenomenon in young children's lives—it's something they notice and wonder about.

A week later Michael made another series of lines, and this time the intentionality was unmistakeable. 'Roads—I ride my cars on them!' he said, showing that he was well aware that marks could stand for real things. He didn't need to draw any cars; in his mind they were already on the roads. His words became part of the drawing as his hand guided the pen.

Events in action are represented in the following drawings by three-year-old Kaya (five months older than Michael). Drawn one after the other, each sheet contains configurations full of meaning. Words tumbled out as she made the first drawing—words about events happening in rapid succession. By the time she made the second drawing she was saying less, but again the movement of her drawing hand drove the narrative. As she filled a large shape with circular pink markings that overflowed in a stream above the shape, she said, 'A volcano's coming out.' It turned out that Kaya knew about volcanos because her grandmother grew up near one in Indonesia, something that had clearly made an impression on her.

Events in action, felt-tipped pens, Kaya (3).

Volcano coming out, felt-tipped pens, Kaya (3). The volcano with erupting pink lava is half-covered by Kaya's left hand.

Geometrical exploration

On another day Kaya wanted to try out a black pen. After making some quick experimental markings and drawing two girl figures, she settled down to make the drawing below left, working with great focus and intensity. As it was clear she didn't want to talk, I remained silent, wondering at the intentions behind her lines as well as the symmetry, order and precision in her placement of shapes. Children's graphic explorations reveal abilities for mathematical thinking—abilities until fairly recently overlooked by educational researchers.

Geometrical investigation is again evident in the exuberant outpouring of ideas shown below right: the mix of geometrical investigation, figure drawings and numerals on a clock face is the product of a mind in action.

Drawing, Kaya (3). The symmetry and order indicate the beginnings of geometrical investigation. That Kaya chose to use only one colour suggests that adding others could have been a distraction.

Drawing, Aden (4). This sheet reflects Aden's rapidly shifting interests as he pursues one idea after another. It may seem to lack order, but take another look at each item separately.

The following examples of playful pattern-making all show an instinct for order—a phenomenon intimately linked to geometrical understanding. You can see it in Matthew's drawing (below left) made the day after watching his first New Year's Eve fireworks display.

Delight in repeating things—whether words in a chant, lining up pebbles in a row, or arranging shapes on a sheet of paper—is a part of children's lives, part of the human desire for order. I was interested to hear about four-year-old Floria's pattern-making from her mother: 'Rainbows seemed to be a theme that she explored over a long time. I think it was arranging bands of colour that interested her. By five, her patterning became more complex.'

Patterns,
felt-tip pens, Floria (5).

All the colours in the sky from the fireworks! felt-tip pen, Matthew (3). Stroke follows stroke: you can appreciate the rhythmical regularity—*the intentionality*—in the repetition of his lines.

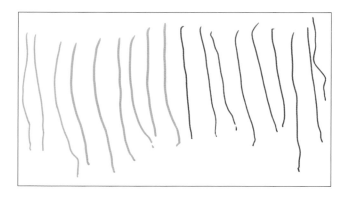

Working in series

Children often work in series, drawing many versions of the same object, topic or pattern that fascinates them. To the casual onlooker it may seem that they are repeating themselves; however, a closer look reveals subtle differences from one piece to the next. Driven by curiosity and a desire for mastery, children may make several different versions of the same thing so as to go deeper into whatever it is that interests them, and to become more skilled at drawing it.

Writhing, wriggling worms in a worm farm so fascinated six-and-half-year-old Persia and her brother, eight-year-old Tyler (who has Down's Syndrome), that they each made drawing after drawing of worms. Despite differences in age and development, they both remained engrossed. When their mother put some worms on a piece of paper so that they could see them while they drew, they became even more engrossed.

Persia was keen to point out details in one of her drawings: 'If you look closely you see little lines on them'. She'd noticed their segmental formation. As well as observing details, it seemed that she was also imagining what it might be like to be and move like an earthworm. 'Look, they're kissing,' she remarked.

Worms (from a series of twelve drawings), felt-tip pen Persia (6). In one drawing (top left), Persia has drawn herself looking at worms with segmented bodies. Enjoying the challenge of depicting intertwined creatures, she's also given them human faces.

Meanwhile, Tyler first made gestural drawings, simply recording the movements of his arm; however, after seeing Persia's drawings, he made a very different drawing (see below). It reminds me of examples of early patterning, but he's also picked up on the wiggliness of Persia's drawings.

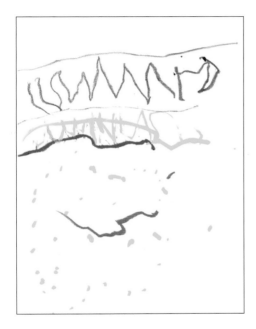

Worms, oil pastels, Tyler (8). The instinct for order in the horizontal bands is striking.

Ever since Anouk saw the tea-party scene in a pop-up book version of *Alice in Wonderland*, she'd been repeatedly drawing tea-party scenes. Below is one of the drawings in which she grappled with the challenge of depicting action within three dimensions. Visualising such a scene is no simple matter.

Girl pouring tea at a tea-party, felt-tip pen, Anouk (5). The tabletop is seen from above with a guest sitting on the right, while on the left a girl bends over to pour tea into a cup (see detail below).

Detail. The girl's arm, curved in an arch, ends with her hand holding the handle of a teapot, which has floral decoration and a fancy lid. Brown tea pours from the spout into a blue mug on the table.

Anouk also delighted in drawing large teapots and teacups. She cut out one of her teapots and a teacup, proudly saying, 'There you are, Mummy, I made you a cup of tea!'

Anouk's cutout teapot was her own invention, inspired by her tea-party drawings.

Teacup and teapot, felt-tip pen, oil pastels, Anouk (5).

Making series of maps of real as well as imagined places has great appeal. 'I like the planning part. It can be whatever you want,' said eight-year-old Timothy.

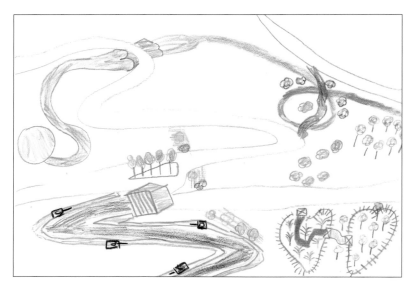

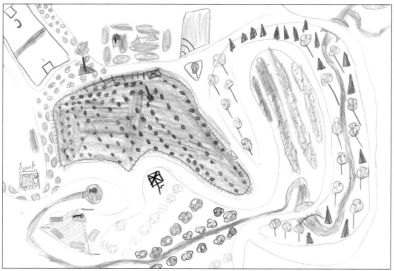

Maps, pencil crayon, Timothy (8). Imagining places with paths, vegetation and bridges over streams was for Timothy a wonderfully calming and playful experience.

Looking at the development in these drawings of faces by Eleanor (that took place over four years), we need to remind ourselves that like other drawings in this book, they were never made for unknown people to look at. Children make drawings out of a deep desire to make sense of their experiences of their world. It's their way of representing their thinking, of making things meaningful to themselves.

Mum and Dad, felt-tip pen, Eleanor (4).

My sister, pencil, coloured pencils, Eleanor (8).

Me, coloured pencils, Eleanor (5).

Portrait of imaginary friend, pencil, coloured pencils, Eleanor (8). Like her previous drawings, this reveals Eleanor's creative response to the essence of what she had remembered and observed.

Responsive drawing: what do you see?

Ruby (nearly six) was on a family camping trip when she suddenly drew a tree quite differently from her usual way. Her mother told me about this 'dramatic change', and to illustrate the difference, showed me one of Ruby's earlier trees drawn from imagination.

Tree, felt-tip pen, Ruby (5). Ruby is finding a way to communicate ideas and feelings about trees–ideas perhaps shaped by memories of storybook pictures.

Tree, felt-tip pen, Ruby (nearly 6). Drawing from observation, Ruby had a chance to sense a tree as a living thing. A chance to create a way to depict fluttering leaves.

At some point experienced drawers like Ruby and Persia in her earthworm drawings, quite independently try drawing objects from life. Ruby had been sitting at a little table with pens and paper in the camping area and simply started drawing the tree. What prompted her? Delight in looking, really looking at a particular tree?

Ruby and the tree she had just spontaneously drawn.

Talking with
Susan Whelan

sw I'm so glad that you talk about valuing the ways children repeat their ideas in series. I've heard people saying things like, *Not again—not more power-rangers, rainbows,* or whatever. Of course it does take time to notice the subtle changes or new details that appear in each fresh version. Children *enjoy* going deeper into a topic. Why does that seem hard for some people to appreciate?

uk I don't think everyone understands that to draw is to explore, to discover. That it's about making ideas visible and trying things out in the way that scientists, architects and artists do. For some non-drawers, drawing means making a finished picture of something seen, remembered or imagined to hang on a wall. It can be that, of course, but often it's not. Sometimes children explore serious issues in series. For instance, Anouk made several drawings about emotional states like being scared.

sw It's easy to be distracted by the fear on the girl's face in this drawing, but I'm fascinated by how much attention to detail has gone into the dragon. Even though the picture explores a negative emotion, it's obvious that Anouk's invested a lot of time in creating this image. But of course not all children want to draw.

uk True. By six or seven years, a lot have competing interests. But it's worth asking why some younger children are reluctant to draw. Sometimes there's a physical reason, like not being able to hold a pen comfortably, or having materials that make only pale marks. Or it could be that children have mistaken notions about what they feel they're supposed to do. I often find that boys tend to become much keener on drawing if they only have black or dark blue pens to use.

sw Perhaps some children feel that drawing doesn't relate to their passions and interests—especially if their experience of drawing has been influenced by older siblings. I remember that my younger son only started drawing in earnest at four when he found that he could draw train tracks. That connected with his passion for trains, so drawing became another way he could enjoy what he loved. Until then, whatever marks he could make didn't hold his attention for long.

Girl scared by flying dragon,
felt-tip pens, oil pastels, Anouk (5).

uk Of course we simply don't know when very young children begin to give meaning to their marks, because they mayn't yet have the words to tell us. Yet even at a very young age they pursue their mark-making intently. They become absorbed in making something happen on a blank sheet of paper and responding to it with further marks, even if only briefly. Once a dialogue starts between a child and the marks [as shown in the photos below], drawing really takes off.

sw I suppose that's why you suggested to Michael that he start drawing by seeing what his pen would do.

uk Yes, appealing to a child's curiosity is always a good idea. Sometimes it can be a mark that's happened accidentally that excites the eye and invites the next mark—surprise often sparks ideas. I remember something John Berger wrote: ... *each mark you make on paper is a stepping-stone from which you proceed to the next* ... [5]

sw Of course when they get older, things become more complex, even frustrating. Like when they want things to look more real.

uk As they may well tell you! You see this shift in approach when experienced drawers start exploring ways to deal with perspective or ways to represent figures in profile, like when Persia drew herself looking at worms.

One mark leads to the next and the next ... What was just a piece of paper has become a play space where anything can happen.

sw What should we do if children ask for help with drawings?

uk I'd try to encourage them to draw alongside another child if possible. I remember overhearing five-year-old Brandon wanting reassurance from his friend Nick when for the first time he drew a profile view of a head. 'I'm only drawing one eye,' he said. 'Yes,' said Nick, 'that's because the other one's at the back of his head.' I'm not sure that experienced drawers really want help as such; sometimes it's more reassurance. After all, children are resourceful and enjoy challenging themselves, so maybe all they really want is acknowledgement that some things are harder to do than others. Whether it's learning to skip, catch a ball or draw in a new way, everything takes practice. By seven and eight, if not before, keen drawers tend to study what other drawers do. So giving them the opportunity to look at illustrations, works of art, advertisements, comics and so on can be helpful. What's important, I think, is to empathise with their intentions if you can.

• • •

As we've seen in this section and previous ones, children use drawing in different ways: as a way of thinking, as a tool to explore possibilities and what ifs—all within a context of play that's entirely their own. I began this section by asking myself four questions: what happens when marks excite the eye? What prompts children's delight in making geometric configurations? What drives them to pursue ideas in series over time? What inspires some to draw things based on observation? While I can't give definitive answers, I hope I've drawn attention to some aspects worth noticing—in particular, visual feedback that delights the eye. This can contribute so much to children's enjoyment in their graphic explorations, which in turn encourages them to persist. And persistence is one key to creative and inventive thinking.

For ways to help younger children when asked, see pp. 95-6.

'Nothing is born of nothing'

The above title comes from the much-loved philosopher and guiding spirit of the Reggio Emilia educational experience, Loris Malaguzzi, who wrote:

'Nothing is born of nothing; everything continues and is transformed. Imagination and logic, as well as feelings, creativity and aesthetics, have a hundred roots and a hundred geneses ...'.[6]

Where do ideas come from?

Malaguzzi's words (translated from the Italian) struck an immediate chord with me when I first read them, because they seemed to sum up vividly and memorably the underlying causes of children's openness to unexpected provocations. Awareness of at least some of the 'hundred roots' helps us to understand and appreciate how children use, supplement and transform whatever they come across. Like all of us, they are drawn to something new; their curiosity is boundless.

Among the many possible experiences and events that may trigger children's imaginations, inevitably some will be distressing. Emotional experiences in a child's life can deeply affect what he or she says or makes: for instance, what inspired five-year-old Anouk's drawing of *Sad Teddy*, crying and bleeding because he fell off his bicycle? Apparently, Anouk was learning to ride a bike at the time. Was this perhaps a troubling experience for her? I still wonder to what extent Teddy was also a projection of Anouk herself. Naturally, we can only speculate about this; nevertheless I feel that the drawing belongs in this book as a clear example of a drawing about feelings.

Over time, Sad Teddy inspired a series of drawings about him in various emotional states.

Sad Teddy, oil pastels, felt-tip pens, Anouk (5). Teddy still wears his crash helmet, tears roll down his face and blood streams from his arms. Perhaps adding such lovingly drawn details made the experience a comforting one for Anouk.

Dancing Teddy with caterpillar hat, oil pastels, felt-tip pens, Anouk (5).

Walt Disney, Joan Miró and Simon

Malaguzzi's words continue to resonate with me when I reflect on an episode that took place years ago in a playroom for two- and three-year-olds. Although an abbreviated version appeared in *Rapunzel's Supermarket*,[7] I include a longer one here because it's a good example of Malaguzzi's 'hundred roots'. I'd lent a book about Spanish artist, Joan Miró, for children to browse through if they wished. Simon (just three, a child who rarely drew or painted) sat down to look at it. As I knew that he liked looking at large adult reference books, quite common in this playroom, I wasn't surprised that he turned over the pages eagerly. I watched closely and said nothing.

The paintings in the book ranged from Miró's early work representing figures and animals, to his later work, filled with biomorphic shapes and calligraphic lines. Simon commented on paintings that contained a lot of black, cheerfully dismissing them as being 'Too scary!' Then suddenly he stopped at one page, utterly riveted. 'Mations! Mations!' he exclaimed, jabbing his finger on it. What was exciting him? I couldn't guess. The painting showed on a deep blue background a bold vertical red line beside a horizontal row of black blobs*. Simon was rapt. Flipping rapidly past other paintings, he constantly returned to this one, repeatedly exclaiming 'Mations!' Later my fellow teacher Janet Robertson showed him plastic animals and learned that 'mations' meant dalmations. That was fine, but why was he so excited? She subsequently learned from Simon's mother that he adored a video of Walt Disney's film *101 Dalmations*, and that his favourite images were ones in which dalmations streak across the screen in a sea of dots.

Shortly after looking at the book, Simon unexpectedly made a painting: three circular shapes in red, yellow and blue in a vertical row beside a vertical line. He then returned to the Miró book, found his favourite painting and said to himself with satisfaction, 'The same'. Although Miró's twelve black blobs are arranged horizontally, not vertically like Simon's, his comment, 'The same', showed an astute awareness: for him his painting reproduced the very features that excited him in the Miró.

Clearly Simon had seen something in Miró's painting that not only connected with his passion for dalmations, but contained imagery that he could use for

* An image can be found on the internet by typing Joan Miró, *Blue II*, 1961 into your search engine.

his own purpose. We can only guess at what this was, but it seems likely that what he wanted to represent was linked to what he'd seen on screen. Was he perhaps trying to represent *non-static* images?

Over ensuing days Simon drew several 'matians'. Significantly, this was perhaps the first time that he used marks to *stand for* something. He'd found a visual language that he could use to make his thinking visible to himself, and to others. I like to think that Miró would have been pleased.

Simon had shown me, yet again, that young children regard certain images with the same curiosity as they do any unfamiliar object of interest: they see them as invitations to action and interaction. It confirms for me the value in offering outstanding picturebooks and other sources of intriguing imagery for them to look through, ponder, and perhaps connect with other aspects of their lives—as Simon was able to do. In finding something in Miró's painting that connected with his passion for his favourite video, he was being genuinely creative.

• • •

So ends Part One and our brief survey of 'the possibilities of things', and some of the 'hundred roots' that may inspire them—examples of what can happen under our noses. I wish to reassure parents and teachers who want 'ideas' for activities that *they* don't need them. Follow the children's lead instead; become their supporter, encourager, and sometimes a co-explorer.

part two

Nourishing and supporting creative thinking

The word 'nourishing' suggests to me the feeding of something alive. However, I have no list of magic ingredients, no magic recipe for nourishing creative thinking; I can only point to some general principles, which I prefer to illustrate with anecdotes rather than presenting them in a list.

'Creativity should not be considered a separate mental faculty but a characteristic of our way of thinking.'

Loris Malaguzzi

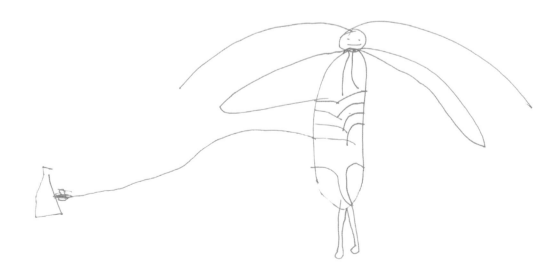

Learning from children

You can't begin to respond supportively to children's spontaneous play unless you believe in its value. Understanding what play is for a child and being able to stand back is what matters.

Being aware that play is a source of wonderful possibilities, which only become apparent once play has begun, can lead you to fascinating discoveries.

'Let's just sit and watch'

I remember well my introduction into the world of early childhood education many years ago. As an artist and newly appointed assistant, I entered a room filled with children at play and asked the teacher/director what she'd like me to do. 'Do?' she asked. '*Do?* I don't want you to *do* anything! Let's just sit and watch.' Then, as we watched the children engaging in pretend play or exploratory play with objects of all kinds, she began to talk about each child with such insight and empathy that I soon learned that until I knew and understood each one, at least a little, I wasn't able to do anything of value.

'It *is* an angel!'

A four-year-old in a kindergarten once taught me an important lesson. Ben was almost up to his elbows in finger paint, moving both hands on a table. 'I making an angel!' he told me. Seeing a similarity to the shape that children make when lying down in sand or snow and moving both arms and legs symmetrically, I unthinkingly said, 'Oh yes, it does look like an angel.' Whereupon Ben drew himself up, stared firmly at me and said, 'It doesn't look like an angel, it *is* an angel!'

Instantly I realised my mistake. Just as I wouldn't say to a child that a cup of pretend tea being offered *looks* like tea, or say to an adult artist that the flowers in her painting *look* like flowers, so I shouldn't have said what I did. While Ben and I were both looking at the angel with joint attention, we were not looking with mutual attention. A subtle but important difference. The difference is one of which I've become increasingly aware since reading child psychologist Colwyn Trevarthen's studies of adult-child relations, and it's something I always try to keep in mind.[8]

When you do manage to tune into children's thinking and free yourself from feeling the need to comment and label, your horizons begin to expand in surprising ways. The more you can learn about children's thoughts, feelings and ideas—and take pleasure in doing so—the more clearly you realise what you can do to encourage curiosity and nurture imagination.

Adults naturally want to 'do things' with children; we want the best for them. Consequently, just watching and listening—without inserting ourselves into the mix—is often not easy. The urge to teach is probably instinctive, but it's also prompted by outmoded ideas about children as 'empty vessels' ready to be filled with knowledge. Over the past several decades, however, an understanding that young children are powerful thinkers and unstoppable eager learners has been displacing this misconception. Yet in our competitive, product-driven world, the idea of allowing children to make sense of themselves and their world through unstructured self-invented play is still too widely ignored.

While I was writing this book, I noticed the cover of a copy of *Scientific American Mind* in my local newsagent; its headline, 'The Serious Need for Play,' jumped out at me.[9] It was disturbing to be reminded that even now the need for play has to be highlighted, despite the extensive literature by psychologists and educators about the benefits of play for children's development. Of course, preschool teachers and many parents firmly believe in the importance of play, but for many other people, play simply means having fun, and is therefore of little consequence. And in today's climate of pressure from policy makers and parents for more structured educational programs with more testing, more assessment and explicit outcomes, play is becoming sidelined even in the early years.

A responsive presence

The warmth of a listening presence does much to keep young children engaged in whatever they're playfully doing. When I'm with under-fives (and particularly with under-threes), whether in small groups or one-on-one, I try to do what researcher, educator and artist John Matthews has described as *a special kind of nothing*.[10] It's a largely non-verbal attentiveness and it works magic in both directions. I become more in tune with the children and more aware of their potential, while my attention encourages them to persist in whatever they're doing far more effectively than words of praise ever could.

Older or more experienced children generally prefer to be watched intermittently, if at all. However, when they trust you to listen rather than take over, they're usually keen to talk about their ideas. At such times, asking about something they've drawn or constructed (e.g. *Can you tell me what's happening here?* or *How does it work?*) can invite conversation. It's important to keep an open mind about their work. Too often our expectations prevent us from seeing what's there to see. When ideas about 'art' cloud our ability to appreciate children's ideas, it's time to remind ourselves that they use visual language as a means of playful enquiry, as a way to understand things.

Taking photographs of children absorbed in play (with their permission) is another way show them that they have your attention, as well as creating a record of events to reflect on later. To discourage them from posing (which interferes with the flow of their thinking), I tell them that I will only photograph them when they're busy.

Reflections to build on

What do the anecdotes in this book reveal about children's imagination? How can we sustain and extend their interests?

Broadly speaking, if we look at what's at the heart of the anecdotes it's possible to find some answers to these questions. Understanding the nature of children's interests is of course key to knowing how you might extend them—your observations are essential.

In this section, I'll try to reach the essence of what lay behind the children's experiences.

Unexpected provocations

From the very first anecdote in this book, when two leaves twirled down in front of three-year-old Michael, it's been fascinating to observe children's alertness to the unexpected, and to see how often the element of surprise can be the catalyst for something new. Children's imaginative responses to unexpected provocations—found objects, enticements of spaces large and small, unforeseen constraints—may lead to unknown territory. Not knowing a destination can be exciting and spurs creativity. When you allow things to unfold without determining outcomes, new possibilities become apparent. And experiencing beauty in the unexpected, as Michael perhaps did with the leaves, was one of those unforeseen moments worth treasuring.

Trying to tease out elements that make imagination blossom is challenging for many of us. But if you're alert to children's responses to the unusual, the unfamiliar, you'll be more in tune with what they do, and able to give them that close and loving attention that nourishes creativity.

I need to make clear, however, that I am not recommending that you provide children with novelty for its own sake. A new material, implement or activity may be interesting or entertaining for a short time, but unless it fits in with children's interests and offers a number of possibilities to pursue, they're unlikely to remain purposefully engaged. And, as we've seen, creative thinking depends on purposeful engagement. Moreover, a steady diet of adult-chosen, one-off activities denies children opportunities to find the extraordinary in the ordinary *for themselves*—as the children we've met in this book were able to do at home.

Underlying complexities

While my anecdotes are unique in their particulars, the ideas underlying them are not. Ideas about family, friendship, other relationships, home, imagined worlds, or good versus evil, which are at the heart of many of them, also underlie much of children's self-initiated and unstructured play anywhere. Anywhere, that is, where children have enough time in the early years to learn how to play imaginatively.

Developing an awareness of the feelings about family and home that underlie children's typical drawings of houses, for instance, allows you to look at such drawings anew and see things more from their perspective. A child's drawing of a house represents more than a literal house: it is 'our first universe', in philosopher Gaston Bachelard's words.[11] From this viewpoint, images like the ones that follow seem to embody feelings about family, home, friendship and safety. The drawings don't depict houses as such: each is about 'house-ness' or home, and also perhaps about 'inside-ness' and 'outside-ness'. What a contrast to the formula-driven exterior view of a house that children are often required to produce!

Drawing, felt-tip pen, Luna (4).
Like a parent with sheltering arms, this personified house embraces all within it.

Sammi (4) tells me she's drawing a roof garden atop her drawing of a house. (The front door of the house is near her left hand.)

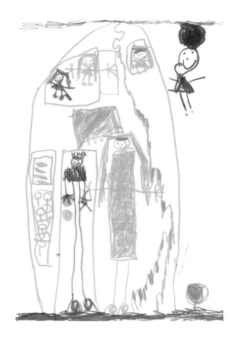

House, felt-tip pen, Floria (4). This drawing seems to embody feelings about family, home, friendship and safety.

Three-dimensional thinking

Whether with blocks, found materials, plasticine, clay, or even upturned furniture, the business of making structures offers children opportunities to think inventively. Working in three dimensions assumes that you'll make something that stands up and, ideally, stays up. It requires you to think imaginatively in different ways. The joy of inventing solutions to construction problems often keeps children deeply engaged. Working three-dimensionally can also lead them to create whole landscapes around themselves, and may inspire imaginative play and story-making. Thus building and narrative can go hand in hand.

The toy as a character

Toy characters often play a role in the anecdotes: manufactured toys such as the teddy bear (page 63) or other stuffed animals (Choochoo and Max, pages 39-41), or self-made ones like the 'worry dolls' (page 42) and the bejewelled crocodile (page 10), or even invisible characters in a miniature paper interior (page 28). Tiny plastic people and animals adorn the wooden *Tower of magic* (page 9) and play their part in a plasticine structure (page 38). Sometimes I'm even inclined to regard vehicles as characters when I see them put to action. These particular examples may remind you of the deep emotional attachment children retain for toys even when they've supposedly outgrown them.

Cartoon characters

Leah tells her grandfather something about Pikachu, a character in *Pokémon,* a Japanese children's television series.

Pikachu, Leah (3). One of five drawings of Pikachu that Leah made one after the other. Drawn from memory in a single contour line, the shape clearly echoes the shape of her toy Pikachu.

By age three, as we saw with Simon and the 'Mations' (page 64), cartoon images may already play a role in children's lives. Their experiences with cartoon characters are not only visual but often tactile as well; they play with toy versions. Making repeated drawings of favourite toy cartoon characters seems to preoccupy some children, and I can see why. With their simple symmetrical shapes, these toys not only invite handling and interaction, but also seem to radiate an energy (good or bad) that speaks to the imagination.

Drawings of them by three- and four-year-olds are interesting because you don't often see children attempt to 'copy' the appearance of objects until they're older. Even more interesting is the fact that such drawings, swiftly made one after the other without looking at the toy, are often made in a single contour line—something again that is generally seen only in older children's work. This suggests to me that frequent handling of certain toy characters can affect children's drawing styles.

Mushu, drawn from memory, Leah (3). Mushu, a small skinny red dragon, is a character from the Disney animated movie *Mulan,* set in ancient China.

To encourage imaginative play with such characters, you might suggest that children cut out their drawings (with or without your help). Cutouts gain a three-dimensional quality that can generate pretend-play and even lead children into inventing characters of their own.

Aliens and alien animals, cutout drawings and toys, Joshua (6).

Alien, Joshua (6).

These carved-out letters never fail to attract 22-month-old Lily's delighted attention.

Alphabetical and numerical symbols

At an early age children become curious about numbers and letters. They begin to notice that their everyday environment is filled with signage.

By age three or four, the initial letter of their name and their age expressed in a numeral hold a special power for children. So it's not surprising that they want to form letters and numbers when they draw, and, as with any new skill, they like to practice making them in various playful ways. Aden's drawings on page 49 show how early attempts at number and letter formation often appear on the same piece of paper as drawings about objects or events. This mixing of different kinds of symbol-making is important developmentally; it's how children begin to acquaint themselves with the grown-up world of symbols. Unfortunately it doesn't always get the recognition it deserves.

Drawing, Aden (4). Typical of the many investigations that children do at home, here's another playful mix of figuration and letter formation that shows thinking in action.

Beginnings of mathematical thought

Another feature to notice is that mathematical thought is often imbedded in early playful graphic exploration. Maulfry Worthington and Elizabeth Carruthers, two educators/researchers who have studied the growth of mathematical thought in children's early years and suggested how adults might nourish and support its development, refer to 'children's mathematical graphics'—a term I find helpful when looking at examples like those below.[12]

Pages from a book, fine felt-tip pen, Paul (4). Made spontaneously and unobserved at home, these 'pages' show Paul's interest in representing his mathematical thinking.

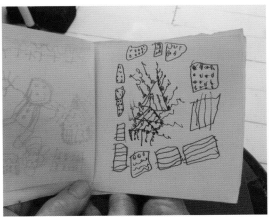

Birds, felt-tip pen, Luna (4).
The thinking that prompted this
sequence of birds is striking.

Drawing, felt-tip pen, Floria (4).
Once you've been alerted to the
idea of 'children's mathematical
graphics', drawings like this
become easier to understand and
appreciate.

Beginnings of pattern-making

Allied to children's mathematical thinking is their self-invented pattern-making. This often seems to start when children draw or paint a row of evenly spaced lines of similar height (as in three-year-old Matthew's drawing on page 50, which may be developed further (as in Zara's pink and purple drawing on page 24).

Having previously written about similarities between musical rhythm and visual pattern-making, I was fascinated to hear about three-year-old Zoe's drawing from a friend who had observed her at a school concert. Zoe was listening from the back of the hall, where she had been doing quiet little dances in time to the music. When she got tired, her mother gave her a sheet of paper and a ballpoint pen to occupy her. She lay down on the floor, and after making a few flowing lines on the paper, started to follow the music by drawing tiny vertical lines in a row *exactly in time.* As the music became louder, so her lines became longer: in other words she was mapping the change in dynamics. It was a wonderful example of what Colwyn Trevarthen sees as young children's innate musicality.[13]

Drawing, ballpoint pen, Zoe (3). A self-initiated drawing of lines in a row made *in time to* music and increasing in size as the music grew louder.

Digital image-making

The making of a storybook about the adventures of Choochoo and Max (pages 39-41) shows one way children can use a digital camera and computer (with some adult help when needed) to make books incorporating images they've devised themselves. Unlike making movies using a digital application that provides ready-made images and special effects—exciting and impressive as these may seem at first glance—the Choochoo and Max storybook shows how children can use technology to create images of their own invention. It's a case study that may interest parents and teachers concerned about the quantity of visual stimulus children receive from digital media, and worried that consequently they are missing out on time for thinking imaginatively—to say nothing of physical exercise.

The compulsive pull of the digital world on young minds could not have been more sharply impressed on me as when I recently watched three three-year-olds in a cafe engrossed in manipulating their parents' smart phones while the parents chatted. What children are likely to use in the future—particularly now that platforms are becoming increasingly portable—and what we are yet to learn about how digital technology affects the formation of young brains, are crucial issues.

'Animated colouring-in books' is how a software engineer recently described to me how she saw much of the digital material that young children currently interact with and manipulate. She thought there was little difference from the old-fashioned colouring-in books that might keep children busy, but never did much to develop their imagination.

However, there are applications (depending on how they're used) that do include possibilities for creative thinking, so that the child becomes an agent, an inventor, and not simply a manipulator. I heard about one such application from Janet Robertson of Mia-Mia Child and Family Study Centre at Macquarie University, Sydney, who kindly gave me the following account.

'We have begun to explore the iPad as a tool for children to make their thinking visible. Rather than using sites or apps which are entertaining, we decided to seek ones which added to children's existing skills, and their desires to draw and draft their ideas.

Explain Everything is the one we chose. You can use it as an interactive screen: it has drawing, recording and voice-over tools which enable children to narrate their story while animating their drawings.

Four-and-half-year-old Kevin drew images of fish to act as characters for his story while other children contributed suggestions. We use a data projector linked to the iPad, throwing a dynamic work-in-progress/action image on the wall for two or three other children to engage with. In this way the work can become collaborative, and the notion of an individual working alone on the iPad is immediately deflated.

Kevin inserted an underwater photograph as a background to the fishy characters, and then animated each fish, including a fearsome shark, whilst telling a tale of a clever eel who escaped the shark—a story which also incorporated suggestions from the other children. As he worked, the presentation was recorded, enabling it to be viewed as a movie later.'

The following photograph shows another story-making and drawing experience in action.

Aidan is using a photo of his block building to re-imagine the game of astronauts he and his brother had played earlier. He uses his finger to draw an additional underwater plot, including an ocean, an octopus and a scuba diver. The iPad enables him to keep on adding details to the photographic and imagined landscape (which he can expand or contract).

Digital story-making

The photograph on the previous page may surprise some of you—as it did me. But what I find most striking about it is that regardless of the digital technology involved, the brothers are doing what children have always done: making up a story about an invented world, a world that is both real and not real.

A significant part of their ongoing story is the original setting: the photograph on the iPad shows a play structure they'd made out of large wooden blocks, a landscape in which they could pretend to be astronauts. With the photograph of this landscape on the iPad, they continued to expand their imaginary world by narrating a continuation of the story as one of them drew with his finger figures and creatures in action.

Inventing a story while simultaneously drawing and narrating is not so very different to what children often do on paper. What is different and what makes it exciting is that the iPad, to use artist David Hockney's words, 'is like an endless sheet of paper ... You can go on and on adding to the drawing.'[14] Children can choose which of the options on offer best suits their purposes. Being able to use a finger to draw with instead of a pencil or marker means that even inexperienced drawers can quickly make complex drawings. Children are encouraged to plan ahead. The fact that the drawing process can be coupled with narration that is recorded, and allows children to expand or contract a drawing and draw things on top of other things, means that play with such an application enables them to find new ways to invent stories.

'It's not about learning how to draw: it's about drawing to learn, drawing to think, drawing to communicate ...' is how artist Pauline Baker sees it. 'It doesn't replace what you can do with paper and pen, it's just another means, another language that can encourage creativity.'[15] I can readily see that for young children this experience is not so much about picture-making as it is about drawing as an endless process of discovery, a new way to communicate stories.

Alright, I've been asked, but does the device provide a valid medium for drawing? While drawing on an iPad undoubtedly extends how and what you can draw in fascinating ways, I don't think that *any* device will ever replace pen or pencil on paper. I recall mentioning in *It's Not a Bird Yet* that architect Frank Gehry, famous for his pioneering use of computers in designing buildings, made the first rough sketches for his marvellous Guggenheim

Museum in Bilbao by hand on some hotel notepaper.[16] Reportedly, he always starts his planning with rough sketches on paper.

I should emphasise that I don't think it's necessary to acquaint young children with electronic drawing, especially if it deprives them of time to draw on paper. However, it will interest many and can lead to inventive story-making.

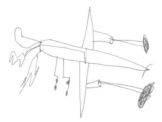

And so we come to end of 'Reflections to build on', so named because whether or not you agree with my thoughts about the anecdotes, I hope that they will give you something to ponder, ideas you might like to extend further.

It's been interesting to see children of their own accord not only inventing imaginative scenarios, but also exploring mathematical ideas, musical ideas and engineering ideas, as well as methods of experimentation and problem-solving. In their separate ways, they can independently pursue interests and passions with great seriousness of purpose for extended periods of time. For them, 'art' is not an optional extra in their lives but a key way, a visual language, for making meaning, for learning about themselves and their world—a world as I noted from the drawing above, that also includes fighter planes.

Young children have remarkable powers to think imaginatively, creatively and independently—as recent research by neuroscientists and leading psychologists like Alison Gopnik has shown.[17] The best we can give children is a supportive environment where they feel their experiments and inventions are valued—where they can try things out, learn to persist when things don't work out, and also feel confident that it's fine in the end if they don't.

Of course all children are different, but then adults are too. So I urge you, whether at home or in an educational setting, to develop your own ways of wondering and imagining, your own creativity in responding with empathy to children's experiences.

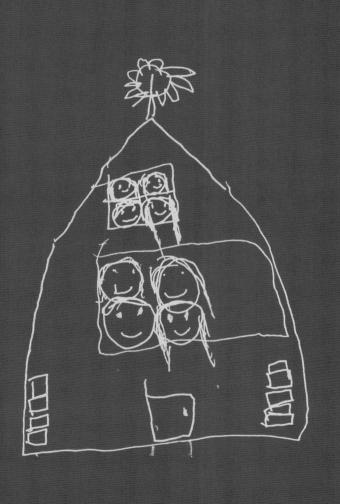

Time, space and materials

The elements of time, space and materials make it possible for children to explore, invent and make their ideas visible. Thinking of these elements as invitations gets to the heart of the matter.

It's the *combination* of unhurried and uninterrupted time, inviting spaces and materials that guides mind and hands, that invites creative thinking. Seeing, handling and thinking are inseparable, as Rudolf Arnheim, psychologist and scholar of art and ideas, reminds us.[18]

Together, time, space and materials provide 'invitations to act'.

Time

Apart from having enough unhurried and uninterrupted time for action and interaction, children need time to wonder, daydream and extend their imagination. When such occasions are shared with an adult companion, they become even more special. Slowing down, doing nothing in particular, helps imagination to flower. In his book *Under Pressure: How the Epidemic of Hyper-Parenting is Endangering Childhood*, Carl Honoré (who coined the term 'slow parenting') pleads for more time for children to wonder.[19] To remind us of what is important in children's lives, he quotes the first four lines of William Blake's poem, 'Auguries of Innocence':

> *To see a world in a grain of sand*
> *And a heaven in a wild flower,*
> *Hold infinity in the palm of your hand*
> *And eternity in an hour.*

In capturing the intensity of a child's gaze, that first line says it all!

Spaces

Working spaces in the anecdotes we've shared varied from kitchen tables and areas on the floor, to outdoor spaces on verandahs and in leafy backyards. They were inviting places where children felt comfortable and a certain amount of temporary disarray was tolerated (though it was understood that children would help with tidying up). The feature common to all was that supplies of basic materials remained permanently in a place from which children could help themselves at any time. While a supporting adult would be in earshot, occasionally coming closer to see how things were progressing, children over four or five years mostly worked contentedly on their own.

Materials

This matter-of-fact heading masks the aesthetic dimension of objects and materials, and how this connects with the movement of the hand and the imagination. Too often we adults focus on techniques, and on having children quickly make something, rather than allowing them time to handle objects and materials, and to savour qualities that can arouse memories as well as spark ideas.

The key to the sustained engagement of the children at the centre of the anecdotes was that they had chosen materials and objects for their own playful and imaginative purposes, and had decided for themselves what they'd do with them. There weren't any 'set-up' activities; rather, in different ways, they responded to the physicality of the materials. The 'feel' in the hand, or the 'look' of appealing colours, initiated a dialogue between child and materials, one in which ideas about transforming the materials into props for pretend play—often along with tiny toys (cartoon characters, animals and vehicles)—soon developed.

Children not only saw potential in things like pearly iridescent buttons to make an image, but also their beauty. Aesthetic responses to materials and objects often played a role in shaping ideas.

Paper—in many different shapes and sizes—is a material that never fails to excite the imagination. Stapling together small sheets of paper to make little books occupied more than one child. Opposite are two examples.

The look and feel of fabric pieces speak to the imagination of nine-year-olds, Darcy and Lilia.

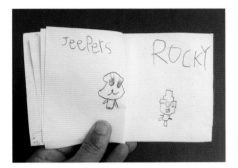

Book of drawings and words,
Joshua (6).

Anna (8) pastes a drawing into a
book of stapled pages to illustrate
a story she typed on a computer.

Among my more surprising finds was a drawing that contained stickers. I'd never thought that such images could encourage creative thinking, but I had to change my mind when I saw four-year-old Sammi's complex drawing. Inspired by twelve tiny round stickers depicting cupcakes that a friend had given her, Sammi imagined an entire scene in a cake shop filled with people buying goodies for Mother's Day. Her drawing shows a counter with the cupcakes in a row. Behind the counter is a central figure with a fancy chef's hat. On either side of her are two assistants (they started off as two decorative hearts before Sammi transformed them into people). Near the top of the drawing, beneath ceiling lights, are five linked figures in a space that's intended to be understood as the background.

Cake shop, felt-tip pen and stickers, Sammi (4). Imagining and creating this scene about shopping for cupcakes for Mother's Day was a wonderfully challenging cognitive experience.

Detail: Cupcake stickers on the counter.

So what do I think about stickers now? Clearly the stickers provided Sammi with an idea; however, as a rule of thumb, I wouldn't provide stickers or other ready-made images for pasting as they generally don't encourage creative thinking.

On the other hand, picture postcards and photographs (particularly those of children themselves, family members or friends), as well as picture books, are good to have around to delight the eye and spark ideas. An onlooker could also offer to sit for a portrait.

Self-portrait, felt-tip pen, Persia (8). An amusing photo of herself with tilting head and crossed eyes prompted Persia to draw this self-portrait.

Grandmother (seated at a table), coloured pencils, Robbie (nearly 7). After a close look at his grandmother's face, Robbie drew her hair and eyes; the rest was drawn from imagination.

What about painting?

My account of experiences in children's homes hasn't included much painting. Why? As a mother of three children under seven explained, the time and effort involved in setting up painting experiences yield smaller returns compared with drawing, cutting, pasting or block-building activities that children can easily engage on their own. I have reassured busy parents that there's no need to feel guilty about not providing painting experiences— provided that children have ample time to draw. After all, drawing, long regarded by many as the poor cousin of painting, is now receiving the respect and recognition it deserves as a powerful way to explore and communicate ideas and feelings. Of course painting can do this too, and gloriously so, but it requires adult care, attention to practicalities, and needs to be offered regularly. A surprisingly good substitute for painting with colours, and easily set up, is painting with water on chalk boards or outdoor surfaces like concrete pathways and wooden fences. Children use the wet brush as a drawing implement, delighting in seeing the surface magically darken where they apply the brush, and then gradually fade.

Pattern, coloured pencils and oil pastels, Floria (5). This doesn't tell a story or describe something seen, but like a piece of music, it has a rhythmic internal order that supports the joyousness radiating from the colours.

Here are examples of three other alternatives which can be easily accommodated at home. Although the first was done with coloured pencils and oil pastels, not paint, it has a painterly feel. In balancing colours in relationship to each other, Floria shows a sense for composing, engaging in what Vea Vecchi calls *aesthetic research*.[20] Floria shows you that keen painters don't always have to have paint!

My second example didn't involve the use of paint either.

Bird, watercolour pencils, Anna (7). Anna stroked a wet brush over her drawing—another simple way to 'paint' without paint.

My third example was done with watercolour paints. When eight-year-old Ishara's pattern paintings were dry, she folded each into thirds. Then, in what you could call 'drawing with scissors', she cut out diamond and lozenge shapes along the folds to make patterns *within* patterns. A lovely idea.

  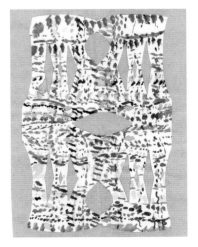

Patterns, watercolour pasted onto backing sheets, Ishara (8).

Ishara starts a new painting using
a fine brush and watercolours.

What prompted Ishara's idea? I don't know, but possibly a tapestry on the wall
or her postcards of patterns on traditional clothing in her native Nepal had
some influence.

And what about clay?

Despite clay being a marvellous material for young children, I've not included
it in this book. As with painting, the practicalities of offering clay regularly
can be daunting for busy families. Plasticine of good quality for older children
and play-dough for younger ones are really not alternatives to clay, but they do
enable children to make things in the round.

Information on claywork, as well as painting and drawing, collage and
construction, can be found in *Rapunzel's Supermarket: All about Young Children
and their Art* (listed under Kolbe) in Further reading on page 105.

Words (helpful and unhelpful)

On previous pages I've written about the benefits of silently watching and
listening when a young child draws; however, I know readers may also like
some tips on useful things to say. Here are some suggestions:

Comment on what you see the child make. For instance, *You're making lots of lines / going round and round / making some big round shapes / making lots of small shapes / using lots of colours, etc.*

Pick up on any words, sounds or gestures a child makes while drawing. For instance, *Yes, I can hear you're making car noises.*

To older children who want your reaction to more complex drawings, you might ask, *Can you tell me what's happening here? How does it work? How did you start? Which bit do you like best?*

Keep in mind:
- that drawings can not only stand for people, animals or objects, but can also represent movements and sounds
- often children's words, sounds and body language will complete an image
- children may explore ideas that change rapidly from mark to mark
- a drawing can be about events occurring in time, more in the sense of a movie than a static image.

Avoid asking *What is it?* This question implies that you expect the drawing to be a certain something. It's been rightly called a 'dead-end question'.

Try not to overpraise. You don't want to encourage children to expect praise for everything they do. Let them enjoy the experience on their own terms. Remember your interested face often says more than words can.

How to help when asked

Sometimes inexperienced children appeal for help with drawing because they don't know how to start. This usually occurs when they want to draw something they've seen peers or siblings draw.

Try suggesting they make a shape (generally they make some sort of circular shape). Depending on what they want to draw—say, a bird—you might ask, *If it's going to fly, what will it need?* As three-year-old Andrew once showed me, as soon as he saw his circular shape, he knew what to add to it: a short line projecting from each side as a wing. On his own he then added a beak (a vertical line at the top of his shape). For him the bird was complete. Similarly, when Danny desperately wanted to draw a fire engine but believed he couldn't, I suggested he start by making a shape. Instead of a shape, he carefully drew a horizontal line, but this didn't matter. 'What will it need to go on the road?', I asked. 'Wheels!' he said happily, and went on to draw a fire engine to his own satisfaction.

If I'd drawn a bird for Andrew or a fire engine for Danny, I wouldn't have helped them at all. If I'd drawn what they wanted in an adult fashion, they wouldn't have been able to use the drawing as a basis to work from, and if I'd drawn in a simple cartoon-like fashion, I'd have given them a formula. Trying to copy a formula devised by an adult can lead to frustration as well as killing the creative spirit. Making drawings according to a formula or a set of instructions places an emphasis on drawing as a skill rather than as a way to think, a way to create something new.

When experienced drawers are unhappy with their drawings, I suggest they start again, or that they try to redraw the part that's troubling them, either on a photocopy of the drawing or on a piece of tracing paper laid on top. If they draw on several sheets of tracing paper, they'll have a number of drawings to choose from. Sometimes just a change from a stubby felt-tip pen to a 2B pencil helps. I always reassure children that it's better to make many drawings of something rather than struggle over one.

If children have trouble remembering how something looks, looking at real objects, pictures or photographs and drawing what they see can open new doors. Observational drawing can delight experienced drawers. It invites them to look closely at things and encourages them to make more detailed drawings. It may also inspire a host of new ideas to explore.

Children's curiosity is unstoppable; through being curious they learn about their world. They explore and experiment with whatever they encounter. As their understanding of people and events in their lives deepens, so they invent new ways to communicate feelings and ideas about their experiences. The more opportunities they have to draw, the more able they become to use drawing as a language in complex and imaginative ways.

Final words

I have two more stories I want to share with you. They celebrate moments, often unnoticed, that speak of the human drive to make something new, something original, something special to the maker.

In this book I've focussed on the visual languages because they encourage imaginative and creative thinking and offer children such powerful ways to make their thinking visible. However, that's not the only way they can enact it.

Ouch-grouch!

Standing in a queue behind a mother and her four-year-old daughter, I witnessed a process of invention take place right before me. Playing with just two words that took her fancy, the little girl began bouncing up and down in time to a made-up chant: *Ouch-grouch! Ouch-grouch! Ouch-grouch!* Within seconds, she took it a step further: chanting *ouch* with an upward inflection and *grouch* with a downward one, while clapping her hands and hopping in time to the new beat. How long this musical improvisation and dance would have lasted, had not she and her mother passed through the check-out, I can't say. Brief as it was, however, this little scene revealed another way a child can imaginatively shape and arrange elements to make something of her own, something that combined sounds, words and movements into a unified whole.

It was another glimpse into the essence of creativity: the joy of playing around and the curiosity to move along unknown paths. It's what scientists do as much as artists, it's what we all can do in any of our chosen endeavours.

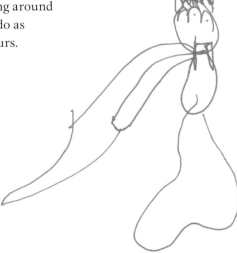

The upside-down scooter

My last story is about something that happened outdoors on a grassy patch bordered by thriving greenery beside a road. There's something about being out in the open and close to growing things that affects wellbeing, that fuels the imagination.

From a short distance I watched a small girl about three or four. Unnoticed by her family bustling around, she bent down to pick up her overturned scooter from the ground. She managed to get it into a vertical position—except that it was upside down, the handlebars on the ground. To her surprise, standing before her was now a triangular frame—her own height—looking like the storybook profile of a pitched roof. To no-one in particular she exclaimed, 'Hey, I made a house!' Gazing at it another second she said to herself with great satisfaction, 'I *made* it!'

The family wandered off, and I was left with another indelible image of a child making an imaginative connection between two unrelated things. I was reminded again of how strongly the image of 'house', and all that it means, is deep within us.

The little girl's response to the triangular frame standing before her reminded me, too, of words by John Berger in his classic *Ways of Seeing*:

> We never look at just one thing; we are always looking at the relation between things and ourselves.[21]

Practical matters

Materials and tools in the home

Easy access for children to materials and tools in a designated spot enables them to make things spontaneously and independently—vital for encouraging creativity.

The range of materials available should never be such that making choices becomes overwhelming. It's far better to have fewer items from which to choose than too many. Having to make do with less can often be a spur to creative thinking.

What is important, however, is that the materials and tools are the best you can afford and in top condition. Worn-out felt-tip pens, blunt pencils or scissors that can hardly cut are uninviting. The quality of the materials and tools is far more important than quantity.

Clear plastic containers or baskets for storing items make it easier for children to find what they want and, importantly, learn to return items when they've finished working. A grocery box for unwanted leftover bits and pieces is useful too.

Listed below are the materials that were available to the children featured in the anecdotes—depending, of course, on their ages and interests.

Basic materials and tools

- non-toxic felt-tip pens (thick and thin) of good quality; short stubby markers for the very young
- non-toxic thick oil pastels (preferable to crayons as oil pastels have stronger colours)
- coloured pencils
- paper in different sizes
- scissors (with rounded tips)
- stapler
- non-toxic glue sticks
- sticky tape
- containers of odds and ends, such as pieces of wood, corks, pipe cleaners, paddle-pop sticks

Extras

- cardboard sheets in various sizes and textures; a long roll of paper
- recycled material such as cardboard containers
- collage materials, e.g. small pieces of coloured paper (matt, shiny, metallic, patterned), tissue paper
- for older more experienced children: non-toxic white wood-working glue, masking tape, soft pencils (2B, 4B or 6B), soft charcoal, watercolour pencils, watercolours (in sets), one or two fine brushes of good quality

Other items

Toys like wooden blocks, vehicles and miniature characters, as well as improvised dress-ups and items such as buttons, can play a role in what children make or depict.

Creative play with natural materials like seed pods, twigs, petals and stones often inspires imaginative ideas.

Things digital

Cameras, computers and iPads, for example, offer children new ways to make images. What's important is to look for programs that enable them to make images that are entirely their own. Manipulating templates designed by adults may be fun, but inevitably limits their imagination.

Wattle twig, 4B pencil, Eleanor (7). In this example of responsive or observational drawing, you can see that with a soft pencil and a real wattle twig in front of her, Eleanor has drawn a sensitive study.

Notes

1. Cynthia à Beckett, 'Imaginative education explored through the concept of playing in the in-between', in T. W. Nielsen, R. Fitzgerald & M. Fettes (eds), *Imagination in Educational Theory and Practice: A Many-Sided Vision*, Cambridge Scholars Publishing, Newcastle upon Tyne, UK, 2010, pp. 191-208.

2. Vea Vecchi, 'Poetic languages as a means to counter violence', in Vea Vecchi & Claudia Giudici (eds), *Children, Art, Artists: The Expressive Languages of Children, the Artistic Language of Alberto Burri*, Reggio Children, Reggio Emilia, Italy, 2004, p. 138.

   Reggio Emilia is a small town in northern Italy where a remarkable educational project has developed over 60 years and is continuing to evolve in more than 30 infant-toddler centres and preschools. Internationally acclaimed for their quality, these public centres and preschools have inspired educators around the world.

3. Ellen Galinsky, *Mind in the Making*, Harper Collins Australia, Sydney, 2010.

4. Anthony Browne, *Silly Billy,* Walker Books, Sydney, 2007.

5. John Berger, *Berger on Drawing*, 3rd edn, Occasional Press, Cork, Ireland, 2008, p. 3.

6. Loris Malaguzzi, *The Hundred Languages of Children*, exhibition catalogue, Reggio Children, Reggio Emilia, Italy, 1996, p. 30.

7. Ursula Kolbe, *Rapunzel's Supermarket: All about Young Children and Their Art*, 2nd edn, Peppinot Press, Byron Bay, NSW, 2007, p. 128.

8. Colwyn Trevarthen, 'Learning about ourselves from children: why a growing human brain needs interesting companions', Research & Clinical Centre for Child Development Annual Report, vol. 26, 2004, pp. 9-44; http://hdl.handle.net/2115/25359

9. Melinda Wenner, 'The serious need for play', *Scientific American Mind*, vol. 20, 2009, pp. 22-29.

10. John Matthews, *Drawing and Painting: Children and Visual Representation*, 2nd edn, Paul Chapman, London, 2003, p. 184.

11. Gaston Bachelard, *The Poetics of Space*, tr. Maria Jolos, Beacon Press, Boston, Mass., 1969.

12. Maulfry Worthington and Elizabeth Carruthers, *Understanding Children's Mathematical Graphics: Beginnings in Play*, McGraw Hill and Open University Press, Maidenhead, UK, 2011.

13. Colwyn Trevarthen; see note 8.

14. Martin Gayford, *A Bigger Message: Conversations with David Hockney*, Thames & Hudson, London, 2011, p. 198.

15. Pauline Baker, artist and studio teacher; personal communication.

16. Ursula Kolbe, *It's Not a Bird Yet: The Drama of Drawing*, Peppinot Press, Byron Bay, NSW, 2005, p. 109.

   John K. Waters, *Blobitecture: Waveform, Architecture and Digital Design*, Rockpool Publishers, Gloucester, Mass., 2003.

17. Alison Gopnik, *The Philosophical Baby: What Children's Minds Tell Us about Truth, Love and the Meaning of Life*, Picador, New York, 2009.

   — 'Scientific thinking in young children: theoretic advances, empirical research and policy implications', *Science,* vol. 337, September 2012, pp. 1623-27.

   Recent ground-breaking psychological, neuroscientific and philosophic developments are leading to a new understanding and appreciation of young children's scientific thinking. Writing about remarkable discoveries of how babies and young children think, Alison Gopnik not only confirms what early childhood teachers have long believed about play, but also suggests that children need more time for play, not less. The trend toward more structured and academic early childhood programs, she argues, 'is misguided.'

18. Rudolf Arnheim, 'Learning by looking and thinking', in *The Split and the Structure: 28 Essays*, University of California Press, London, 1996, pp. 113-119.

   I came across Arnheim's writing when I started working with children. His idea of the importance of paying attention to the intertwining of seeing, handling and thinking that is at the root of the artistic process coincided with my own and has continued to guide me ever since.

19. Carl Honoré, *Under Pressure: How the Epidemic of Hyper-Parenting is Endangering Childhood*, Allen & Unwin, Sydney, 2008, p. 13.

20. Cited in note 2; the reference here is to p.39.
   Although the authors use the terms 'compositional research' and 'aesthetic research' in the context of arrangements using found materials, I find they also apply to children's pattern-making with drawing media or paint.

21. John Berger, *Ways of Seeing*, BBC, London, 1972, p. 9.

Further reading

Edwards, Carolyn, Gandini, Lella, & Forman, George (eds) *The Hundred Languages of Children: The Reggio Emilia Approach—Advanced Reflections*, 2nd edn, Ablex Publishing, Greenwich, CT, 1998.

Gandini, Lella, Cadwell, Lynn, Hill, Louise, & Schwall, Charles (eds), *In the Spirit of the Studio: Learning from the Atelier of Reggio Emilia*, Teachers College Press, New York, 2005.

Gopnik, Alison, *The Philosophical Baby: What Children's Minds Tell Us about Truth, Love and the Meaning of Life*, Picador, New York, 2009.

Kolbe, Ursula, *It's Not a Bird Yet: The Drama of Drawing*, Peppinot Press, Byron Bay, NSW, 2005.

—*Rapunzel's Supermarket: All about Children and Their Art*, 2nd edn, Peppinot Press, Byron Bay, NSW, 2007.

Matthews, John, *Drawing and Painting: Children and Visual Representation*, 2nd edn, Paul Chapman, London, 2003.

Reggio Children, *The Wonder of Learning*, www.thewonderoflearning.com/?lang=en_GB

Rinaldi, Carlina, *In Dialogue with Reggio Emilia: Listening, Researching and Learning*, Routledge, New York, 2006.

Robertson, Janet, 'Making thinking visible', in Wendy Schiller (ed.), *Thinking through the Arts*, Harwood Academic Publishers, Sydney, 2000.

Schwartz, Louisa & Robertson, Janet, 'Materials matter: a conversation on matters material,' in Alma Fleet, Catherine Patterson & Janet Robertson (eds), *Conversations: Behind Early Childhood Pedagogical Documentation*, Pademelon Press, Mt Victoria, NSW, 2012, pp. 170-87.

Vecchi, Vea & Giudici, Claudia, (eds), Children, Art, Artists, the Expressive Lanuages of Children, the Artistic Language of Alberto Burri, Reggio Children, Reggio Emilia, Italy, 2004.

Vecchi, Vea, *Art and Creativity in Reggio Emilia: Exploring the Role and Potential of Ateliers in Early Childhood Education*, Routledge, London, 2010.

Weisman Topal, Cathy & Gandini, Lella, *Beautiful Stuff! Learning with Found Materials*, Davis, Worcester, MA, 1999.

Worthington, Maulfry & Carruthers, Elizabeth, *Understanding Children's Mathematical Graphics: Beginnings in Play*, McGraw Hill and Open University Press, Maidenhead, UK, 2011.

Index

Train on hills, felt-tip pen,
Matthew W. (5).

Also by Ursula Kolbe

Published by Peppinot Press

It's Not a Bird Yet: The Drama of Drawing, 2005.

Rapunzel's Supermarket: All about Young Children and Their Art, 2nd edn, 2007.

Published by Early Childhood Australia

Clay & Children: More than Making Pots, 1997.

Drawing and Painting with Under-Threes, with Jane Smyth, 2000.

Ursula Kolbe is a Sydney-based artist with 40 years of experience in early childhood education as a teacher, university lecturer, writer, filmmaker and speaker. Her publications include books, articles, films and videos about the arts and young children.

Photo: John McRae

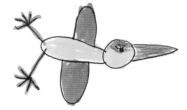

Dreaming of horses, felt-tip pen,
Naomi (6).